A PASTOR'S POETRY
VOLUME ONE

To Rev. Clarence Laney, Jr.,
My Big Brother, Keep the Faith!
Thanks so much for your love and
support through the years.

Yours,
(signature)
December 21, 2005

A PASTOR'S POETRY
VOLUME ONE

KENNY J. WALDEN

A production of
Arts In Religion

Check out our website:
www.artsinreligion.com

Aventine Press
1023 4th Avenue, Suite 204
San Diego, CA 92101

ISBN: 1-59330-327-0

Library of Congress Control Number: 2005908875
Library of Congress Cataloging-in-Publication Data
A Pastor's Poetry: Volume One/Kenny J. Walden

DEDICATED TO MICHELLE

TABLE OF CONTENTS

CHAPTER TWO:
LETTERS FROM A PASTOR'S DESK

CHAPTER THREE:
A PERSON IN A PASTOR

FOREWORD

" ... I will pour out my spirit on all flesh;
your sons and your daughters shall prophesy,
your old men shall dream dreams,
and your young men shall see visions."
(Joel 2:28 RSV)

God pours the Holy Spirit upon young and old enabling them to speak.

John's gospel has a majestic, poetic beginning in which we hear an echo of an earlier text, Genesis 1:1, "In the beginning, when God began creating the heavens and the earth ..." There are gods who create worlds by having sex with other gods, or through a primal, cosmic battle between good and evil, chaos and order. This God creates through nothing but a word. All this God has to do is to say the word, "Light!" and there is light. "Animals!" and there is now something where before there was nothing but formless void.

In the Bible, word precedes world. There is nothing until there are words to create something. Reality is linguistically constructed. Word precedes world. Words do not arise from things, but rather things are evoked by the Word. Word precedes all things. God said, "Let there be light." And there was. Yahweh allowed the earthling, Adam, to enjoy a bit of divine creativity by naming some of the cattle and birds (Genesis 2:20). Creativity is a word-derived phenomenon.

And then, there came One among us, born as we are born, who was named Emmanuel, God with us, Word Made Flesh. And what did he do? He came preaching (Mt. 4:17). Luke records his first great assault upon the world-as-it-is was in a Synagogue, in a pulpit, quoting his favorite prophet, "The Spirit of the Lord is upon me to preach the good news ..." (Lk. 4).

The Word Made Flesh was the embodied, active Word, healing the sick, embracing the untouchable, enlightening the blind, turning over the temple tables, and riding into Jerusalem in triumph. But mostly he spoke. He assaulted the world, not with violent deeds but with a barrage of words – parables that shocked, evoked, amused, and disclosed; sermons that often ended with a riot; blessings, curses, proverbs, and prophesies. He said he brought a new kingdom and some – not that many, not many of the wise and powerful, but enough to attract the worried attention of the authorities – hailed him as "King." He sure talked often enough of his present and coming "Kingdom of God," but that was about all he did to inaugurate his reign. He talked.

Because he is a preacher, Kenny Walden has had to be something of a poet. He is a worker in words. Even as God works a world through words, so Kenny has worked. In this book you will have the adventure of looking over the shoulder of a man who has been given some good words. We preachers have few tools in our pastoral bag of tricks other than words.

In Kenny's reflections we witness a preacher under construction, a young man who is gripped by a grand vision of God's promised future, and a fully alive human being who is, in these honest, eloquent, Spirit-filled words, a sign of God with us.

Any preacher who is faithful to the call of the God of Israel and the church has got to be a poet, to some degree. Kenny's wonderful words help point the way.

William H. Willimon
Bishop of the United Methodist Church
North Alabama Conference

INTRODUCTION

I first met Kenny Walden, an aspiring and inspiring young minister, at a church related conference in Houston, Texas. We solidified the budding relationship at other church related conferences the same year. Every older Pastor, I believe, would like to be known for mentoring someone on his or her journey toward professional ministry in the United Methodist Church. I have had more than my share of such relationships in my many years of service at the General Board of Higher Education and Ministry, as an Annual Conference Council Director and as a Pastor. I am proud to contribute in mentoring Kenny.

Kenny is an intelligent, talented preacher with a burning desire to serve Jesus Christ as an effective pastor. Everything he does, from his appointments as Associate Pastor to his continuing academic studies, is geared toward being an effective 21st Century pastor. What a delight to discover young clergy who understand their call to be one of quality preparation for God's people! They do their best to give the people of God their best.

One feels and reads Kenny J. Walden's aspirations and insights in every chapter of his first book. It consists of two parts, poetry and one part prose. Chapter One and Chapter Three are poetic and Chapter Two is excellent social commentary. It is a marvelous first attempt to put in words what has taken root in ones soul. Bare his soul is what Kenny does in these all too short renderings of his personal and professional journey.

It is clear Kenny reeks with the culture of the Black Church. From his battle with "Short Skirts in the Front Pew" to his insights about "Sunday School" one knows that he personally has been there and done that. The Black Church encouraged learning contrary to some myths in the larger society.

The many poems about African-American church culture are a must to be read. If you were reared in that culture so many things will register in your spirit that a smile will spread across your face from the beginning to the end of the chapter.

It is in Chapter Two you experience his coming of age and his thorough preparation for the 21st Century. Although brief this chapter grounds his values not just as an African-American man but also as an American man. He is as thoroughly rooted in the African-American experience as he is in the American experience. His two-ness is lifted up and exposed in a way that affirms all of life. He is in the words of Eric Fromm a "biophilos" person. A lover of life! Then when he passionately brings together his crafty reasoned understanding of the church and the military, we are ushered into a new era. Some talk about it but he puts it out there. Does this make him a "necrophilos" man as well as a "biophilos" man? You struggle with it. He does!

In Chapter Three you feel and hear his metamorphosis. He is the American Dream talking the talk and walking the walk; "*Father to Son*," "*Father to Daughter*," and "*Bourbon Street*." All of life belongs to him and he belongs to all life. Kenny's first book should be required reading for parishioners, pastors, seminarians, and students of literature and/or religion. One can get a bird's eye view of the Black Church experience while at the same time looking at the soul of a young 21st Century clergyman. He is a different, yet sterling, model of what may be the unique expression of more African Americans to come.

Douglass Fitch
Senior Pastor of Glide United Methodist Church
San Francisco, California

CHAPTER ONE
CHURCH LIFE

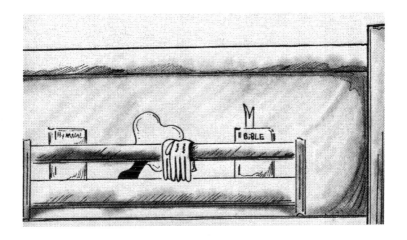

"Try not to become a [person] of success but rather try to become a [person] of values."

- Albert Einstein

A PASTOR'S SATURDAY
BEFORE SUNDAY'S SERMON

Saturday morning,
Thinking about tomorrow's Sunday sermon,
The scripture, the text, the biblical characters,
The introduction, body, and conclusion,
Three points, main points, side points, display of an illusion, or
possible confusion,
Voice pitch, body gestures, illustrations of stories,
Emphasis on God's grace, faithfulness, and mercy.

Saturday afternoon,
Thinking about tomorrow's Sunday sermon,
The scripture, the text, the biblical characters,
The sermon's title, the choir's songs, prayers to be prayed,
Hope growing, hope absent, hope that is decayed,
Saints, seekers, and sinners,
Experienced, doubters, and beginners.

Saturday night,
Thinking about tomorrow's Sunday sermon,
The scripture, the text, the biblical characters,
Asking for divine guidance to help direct God's creation,
Different genders, classes, and nations,
Praying for God's Holy Spirit to do what only it can,
Elaborating, discerning, meditating, and desiring me,
And the rest of the church to better understand.

A PULPIT'S VIEW

At first glance I see,
Men wearing ties and suits, women in dresses and wearing hats,
Babies in diapers, little boys in penny loafers, and little girls' hair plaits,
Deacons or deaconesses, stewards or stewardesses, and trustees at
their familiar position,
Hugs, hand shakes, smiles, nods, squeezes, and some kissing,
Young, middle age, and old,
Gather in the summer's heat, spring's rain, fall's autumn, and winter's
cold.

At second glance I see,
Smiles, frowns, faces of despair and hope,
Parents holding babies, teenagers pulling or tapping on one another's
coat,
Some men sitting with men, some women sitting with women,
Ears wanting to hear sins denounced, other ears wanting to hear sins
forgiven,
People singing, people praying, and people not doing anything, but
wanting to do both,
Feelings full of happiness, sadness, and some full of loathe.

At third glance I see,
Souls searching, minds questioning, human beings wondering about
their after lives,
Sons, brothers, fathers, husbands, daughters, sisters, mothers, and
wives,
Miracles in the past, present, and unfolding,
Faith birthing, growing, and molding,
Talking, yelling, whispering, and signaling,
God's Holy Spirit moving, shaking, dwelling, inspiring, stirring, and
thrilling.

SHORT SKIRTS IN THE FRONT PEW

Trying to concentrate to be an instrument for our Lord and Savior,
Sitting in the chair saying a silent prayer,
Waiting to see signs sent from up above or a message I can hear,
Yes God, all right Lord, but please come in clearer,
Your servant is trying to look and listen only to you,
My eyes scan over the people for religious clues,
Then to my surprise see short skirts in the front pew.

The church is a holy place, not a disco or striptease place,
I do not mind looking at you above the shoulders, but not below the waist,
You can cover your body with clothes and still look classy with lots of taste,
I am trying not to look in your direction as if my eyes are going to get sprayed with mace,
I almost feel out of place, because I am trying to focus on the divine,
Not look up at your behind, you may look a little fine, but this is not the place or the time,
Close your legs, put a cloth over those thighs, cover your chest, and please be kind.

I am trying to do my job and spread God's word,
If someone told you that your appearance is cute, sexy, or fun, just forget what you heard,
I am not trying to abuse you sister about the way you are dressed,
My intention is to ensure that you are going to be blessed,
I guess, but yet I really know, that your body is more than a garden tool,
You are already a jewel, I thought you knew,
There is no need for you to become one of the short skirts in the front pew.

CHURCH BUILDINGS

Brick, wood, and stone to name a few,
Store fronts, gothic, high steeples, traditional, and as contemporary as
me and you,
On highways, dirt roads, side streets, main streets; in cities; on islands,
on mountains, on Beaches, and other places,
Black, brown, yellow, tan, orange, and white faces,
Big, small, short, and tall preachers alike,
Open morning, noon, and night,
Rude, friendly, but hopefully consistently loving and polite.

CHURCH AND STATE

Are Church and State separate?
Can the two ever be?
I noticed the church active in politics early in the Old Testament,
With Moses going to one of the top political figures,
Pharaoh, saying, "Let My People Go."
I observed how some states officially or unofficially declared a
particular religion.

Are Church and State separate?
Can the two ever be?
I have read in the Holy Scriptures how God blessed and cursed several
states,
I have seen many states call on God's intervention for their political
affairs,
I believe that the two are an effective pair when working on the same
page,
Do you think the two are compatible?

Are Church and State separate?
Can the two ever be?
I have studied the churches which gave birth to some of the most
prolific political figures, Such as Dietrich Bonhoffer, Martin Luther
King, Jr., Pope John Paul II,
And Mother Theresa,
I have witnessed states make personal and public appearances in the
church begging,
For a collaboration, or simply votes-mostly votes.

Are Church and State separate?
Can the two ever be?
Do you want to be in a church that ignores or has no relationship?
No contact with the state?
How would that church appear?
How would that state function?

CHURCH CONFLICT

Who is sitting in my pew, because that is my space in the sanctuary?
Is that person the only soloist we have in the choir?
Is tithing my salary really biblically necessary?
Why do the Sunday bulletins have so many announcements?
Are people blaming too many problems or sins on their adversary?

Pastor, I am the only one who is qualified to occupy this leadership position,
My family helped build this church a long time ago,
When is the committee going to make a decision?
I attend worship services come rain, sunshine, sleet, or snow,
Everyone working within a ministry area does not have a gospel mission.

Must we sing every verse in each hymn?
When my parents were sick, no one came to visit them.
We need to change the church carpet's color,
Do I or we have to love all of our sisters and brothers?
Church conflict takes place both in the open and undercover.

SPIRITUAL AWAKENING

I discovered that my being is more than ashes to ashes and dust to dust,
Made of much more than clay vessels that get bumped and bruised, and decay,
With muscles that flex, bones that bend, and a mind that imagines,
I realized a divine presence much bigger than my human experience,
That divine spiritual existence validates mine.

I acknowledge that this life on Earth is merely temporary,
It is not wise to expend all of our time and talents on materials that will surely fade away,
I desire an eternal horizon that is far from contemporary,
It is good to thank God for today and trust God for tomorrow.

We are whole beings, who are made up of a body, mind, and spirit,
I only have one body, so I must respect it; but it, too, will eventually diminish,
It is essential to cultivate my mind the best I can,
But it, too, will dwindle away into erosion,
My spirit can not be eliminated, not even from a nuclear explosion,
I will allow my spirit to live now and forever.

SPORTS... A RELIGION?

A body of people with different talents, on one accord working toward
one mission,
Seeking harmony and peace in their particular area,
Accepting loses together while focusing on winning,
They know what is really going on even if it reflects total hysteria,
Keeping the power of hope even if it appears to be dimming.

I have seen anger, disappointment, frustration, and sheer joy in the
midst,
Hand shakes, hugs, tears, moans, laughter, bursts of shouts,
Of victories and tribulations, rarely do the participants, and future
generations forget,
When it looks as if the whole world is against, still some will not
doubt,
There are rare souls that raise up to refuse to give up and quit.

A WEDDING

Two worlds that have collided, coming together to make one,
Two families in the world attempting to make another,
Two souls in the universe living as one,
Two experiences, ideologies, and philosophies agreeing to live in a
civil union,
Two people saying, "I do," "I promise," and "I will,"
Two minds thinking about the next days, weeks, months, years, and
forever,
Two hearts pounding and praying that this day will be the
beginning of a beautiful life.

ALTAR CALL

Eternal God, we your creation invite your Holy Spirit in this place,
Not only enter this building, but also our hearts, minds, souls, and our most sacred space,
We need your righteous touch upon our lives,
Help make us become responsible brothers, sisters, friends, husbands, and wives,
We approach the altar full of humility,
Realizing we can not come without your grace and mercy, or not come at all,
Come one, come all, to this altar call!

You urge the poor, rich, sick, weak, and whomever to commune with you,
It does not matter the nationality, gender, race, color, or hue,
Assist us to be on one accord seeking justice, peace, harmony, and love,
Resist us to travel this journey without having to push or shove,
Knowing that our strength is not coming from within, but ultimately from above,
Give us the endurance for various challenges no matter how small, big, or tall,
Come one, come all, to this altar call!

When we have ran our last race and can run no more,
When we have taken our last step, opened our last door,
When we have closed our earthly eyes never to see through them again,
Be forever our God, our Lord, our Savior, and our best friend,
To you who is able to keep us from the hellish fall,
We ask for a home in your Heavenly kingdom beyond the moon, sun, and stars,
Come one, come all, to this altar call!

AN OFFERING

You can not beat God's giving no matter how you try!
Will a man rob God?
Store your treasures in heaven and not on earth,
We would rather get the money that fold than jingles,
Give your offering in Jesus' name,
10 percent of your gross,
The love of money is the root of evil.

CHURCH CHOIRS

Sometimes songs can move us in a way that only songs can,
Church choirs amplify heavenly proclamations for all to hear,
When you get in tune with the church choir you will definitely
understand,
They can miraculously calm your worst fear,
You can find them in the evening during the week at their churches
practicing.

The vessels for songs from up above to reach us here below,
There are few musical assemblies that have that spiritual power,
Able to make you warm inside when the outside is freezing with
snow,
You may enter the church feeling small, later feeling like a tall strong
skyscraper tower,
After hearing one of those gospel church choirs.

People singing in unison, sometimes duets, solos, or in two and three
pieces,
Stirring the congregation up as if it was a bowl of soup,
Church choirs are made up of brothers, sisters, moms, dads, nephews,
and nieces,
In some cases helping the preacher's preparation for that heavenly
hoop,
God bless those church choirs.

HOLY BIBLE

It is one book that is made up of many that tells of generations that was, is, and yet to be,
It has books, letters, and gospels for the eyes to see,
It is useful if you loose your mind or your heart starts to bleed,
If you are imprisoned, follow the biblical route, and it will make you free,
It comes in almost every language under the sun,
It has millions of congregations,
Most of them use it to make religious proclamations.

As I turn to the Old Testament pages I discovered my history, which began in the book,
Of Genesis 1:1 when noted, "In the beginning God created the Heaven and the Earth."
I learned and received the laws for my life in the next book called Exodus 20:1-20, Beginning "And God spake all these words, saying…"
I was informed of giving back or tithing to God in the book of Leviticus 27:32, "And, Concerning tithe of the herd, or of the flock, even of whatsoever passeth under the rod, The tenth shall be holy unto the Lord."
I see reflections of my emotions when I thumb through the pages within Psalm 17:1, "Hear the right, O Lord, attend unto my cry, give ear unto my prayer,
That goeth not out of feigned lips."
The New Testament begins with the gospels Matthew, Mark, Luke, and John telling the, Story of my Lord and Savior Jesus Christ "born in a manger,
Because they had no room in the inn."
The Holy Bible ends and continues with the book of Revelation 1:3, "Blessed is he that, Readeth, and they that hear the words of this prophecy, and keep those things which are, Written therein; for the time is at hand."
Constantly praying for discernment of the scriptures so I will better understand.

I go to the Holy Bible for wisdom, comfort, and direction,
It gives me peace, happiness, and protection,
I turn through the pages and it helps take me through this world, in which we live,
If someone needs a holy bible, do not hesitate to offer one to give,
This book is like no other, so pass it to all the sisters and the brothers,
Read about how, when, and why you were created,
And if you spend time reading the holy bible you will greatly appreciate it.

COMMUNION

The body that was broken for us,
The blood that was shed for us,
We receive them both unworthy and in total awe,
May we exist in this world as a living sacrifice.
For the one who paid the ultimate price.

Let all partake of this sacrament from young to old,
The price was paid for everyone, to help save our souls,
It can free you and help your soul to unfold,
You can not be too young and you can not be too old,
No matter how warm I am it brings spiritual chills down my spine as
if it were cold.

I shall forever drink of the cup as long as I shall live,
May all of us bless God's Holy name,
I shall forever eat of the bread as long as it will give,
The cup and bread were given through so much pain,
Let us be proud of communion and never be ashamed.

MEMORIAL SERVICES

There are many religious ceremonies that affect the heart in a variety
of ways,
You may only like attending religious or spiritual services at morning,
noon, or night,
Memorial services tend to linger in one's memory for many nights
and days,
Memorial services usually help bring a peaceful closure to deaths,
But do not necessarily make them right,
I usually like for them to end with an inspirational emphasis so it gives
the possibility of, My soul to fly high like a kite.

We attend memorial services for all sorts of people,
Who were taken away from us for one reason or another,
We get an opportunity to acknowledge their presence in the world in
which we live,
Some of them were famous, ordinary, young, or a sister or a brother,
There is no measurement of value to which they gave,
They are physically dead to us, but their contributions still give,
No matter how many I have attended in the past,
It renders me a chance to consistently discover.

Life is a gift that we receive each day while other individuals in the
African Slave Trade, German Holocaust, American Race Riots, Global
Religious Genocide,
Among many others had their lives tragically taken,
To attend them it takes a certain amount of wisdom, understanding,
and courage,
They take place all over the world in respect, rage, disappointment,
compassionate, kind, And sometimes presenters are somewhat
shaken,
But there is much to be thankful for to acknowledge, appreciate,
remember, and reflect, During a memorial service, so do not be
mistaken.

PASTORAL COUNSELING

God help me to listen to your people's sentences then speak the correct words,
How long have you been beaten by your husband?
How long have you been cheating on your wife?
You are 17 years old and how long have you been seriously,
Thinking about taking your own life?
How long have you resented your parents?
How much money did you lose?
What is the difference between heaven and hell?

God help me to listen to your people's sentences then speak the correct words,
All right Brother, prayer does change things, but sometimes God intends to change us,
All right Sister, keep your hands in God's hands and God will keep you,
Sometimes we have to go beyond the four walls of the church building to have church,
Deaths are not the end and thank God for memories that live on in our lives,
We live to die and die to live again in another life,
Forgiving does more for the victim than the oppressor, so do not live your life oppressed.

God help me to listen to your people's sentences then speak the correct words,
You need to read the book of Job in the Holy Bible,
We all need to read the Holy Bible,
You need to pray about that and we all need to pray more,
I am going to refer you to someone and a place I know and trust,
Let us end in prayer until next time,
God help me to listen to your people's sentences then speak the correct words.

PRAYING MOTHERS

This is for all the praying mothers who decided to carry their child for nine months Pregnant... while praying to God for the world to change, get better, or for the wisdom to Pass to the unborn child... in order for the yet born to accomplish not only survival, but For success to be an attainable goal for the future generations.

This is for the praying mothers who supported their little child in athletics, music, Academics, and other performing arts... sending or taking their little one to practices and Attending events by themselves, with their husbands, or not at all... because of work Demanding their presence but they were still able to be the number one fan.

This is for the praying mothers who prayed their child through puberty, high-school, College, jail, and prison... and knew, hoped, and believed that their child was more than The negative stereotypes projected on radio, television channels, in magazines, and Books... that insulted, overlooked, and ignored their beauty and intelligence.

This is for the praying mothers who constantly, unapologetically, and reverently prayed To God knowing that their cry of help, hope, despair, and thanksgiving was heard by the Creator of all....they were also created therefore making them a unique, valuable special Member of the creation family... they would not allow themselves or their children to Forget the power of prayer.

SINGLES MINISTRY

There is not anything odd about being single; it is actually a blessing,
Believe me there is more to life than a wedding,
You have an entire world to explore and that is far from boring,
Spread your wings and start soaring,
You are far from boring; bring the bible and a few other books so we
can begin touring.
The holy bible highlights the sacredness of singleness and its purity,
One of the most unique groups within the church is the singles
ministry.

Singles are special and rare, some people can not operate independently,
So they must become a pair,
Singles have the ability to be more focused,
Yet they have a plethora of possible distractions,
The church must use its' resources, time, energy,
And finances toward their Singles and take positive actions,
To help ensure that they feel valued, in place, and feel a strong sense
of satisfaction,
The church needs to proclaim the power of one,
The sanctity of becoming priests, monks, and nuns,
There exists a beautiful liberty in the Christian singles ministry.

We were created not in pairs, but each of us created by our creator,
We need not another individual to validate our relationship with our
Lord and Savior,
I celebrate singleness in Jesus Christ of Nazareth,
To him I dedicate my time, energy, and my breath,
I will use my God as my companion, my guide for all eternity,
I thank God for ministering to the singles community,
Let every church create a singles ministry.

YOUNG ADULT MINISTRY

The time is never too late or too early to begin a relationship with our creator,
Many people, places, and things are vying for your time, energy, and attention,
The time is always right to establish and nurture your relationship with our savior,
If not careful some people, places, and things can be a religious or spiritual prevention,
It will help if you attend bible studies, worship services, and pray.

Surround yourself with positive people and energetic ideas so you can gracefully mature,
You can have a lot of fun becoming a Young Adult Christian,
Do not rebuke wisdom or discipline, but righteousness and justice you should adore,
Going to a movie, concert, play, dance, or sport event is not a sin,
Make your spirit rich in the word of God and not poor.

God relates and uses the young just as much as the old,
Read about David and Goliath and Mary the Mother of Jesus to name a few,
There is no friend like Jesus Christ, if you have not been already told,
God forgives, supports, and will turn your old gloomy clouds bright and new,
Join and/or support the Young Adult Ministry, and you will not be left out in the cold.

REVIVALS

People gathered from far and near listening for spiritual messages to hear,
Pastors and preachers scheduling their calendars six months to a year,
Asking God to revive them first to help revive the congregations in solemn prayers,
They take place in storefront churches, cathedrals, high steeple churches,
In cities, and small towns alike,
They are scheduled in the morning, afternoon, evening, or late at night,
If you are feeling down, all of them should lift your spirit up,
Do you want to go? Do you need to go? Let us go to a revival.

It does not matter what Christian denomination,
I just need to hear about Jesus Christ offering an eternal spiritual salvation,
The other attendees can be representing any ethnicity, race, gender, or nation,
I need a word from heaven to help me live here on earth,
Love, peace, hope, and faith, among other virtues I want the revivals to give birth,
I will drive, ride, walk, catch a bus, and maybe even a taxicab,
Do you want to go, do you need to go? Let us go to a revival.

At the revival I want to hear the piano play to confusion,
Whatever the problems are I want the drums, organs,
And tambourines to help find a solution,
I want to have a hands clapping, foot stomping, holy ghost good time,
Move out of the way clouds, because here comes the sunshine,
If my attendance at revivals is wrong, I will have to commit the crime,
I am not going to complain about the summer, winter, spring, or fall,
Do you want to go, do you need to go? Let us go to a revival.

PREACHERS

Preachers are multi-talented, play many roles and wear several hats,
They should be familiar with foreign affairs, national,
And local news from the neighborhood laundry mats,
They will hear a variety of information from their parishioners,
And other people who make up their congregation,
They will get stopped by people wanting their attention in the grocery
stores,
Malls, and the local gas stations,
They are unique, special, rare, but their type can usually be found in
every nation.

There are rare moments when preachers can lay back and not be a
preacher or priest,
Those moments are priceless and far in between to say the least,
Preachers must pray night and day and remember to never cease,
It is important to remember that preachers are also people who are sons,
daughters, Mothers, fathers, brothers, sisters, uncles, and nieces.

Preachers may come in any size or shape,
Some wear robes, suits, shirts, ties, collars, or may use a cape,
At any rate they attempt to successfully navigate through a religious
and spiritual quest,
They may come from or reside in small towns, big cities, north, south,
east, or west,
It does not matter where God has placed the preachers; they will try
their very best.

PARISHIONERS TO PASTORS

When life circumstances get rough and difficult to bear,
Pastors we need to hear one of your gospel prayers,
When my world tuns upside down and I am experiencing my darkest night,
I need to hear one of your sermons reminding me that Jesus Christ will make things right,
Parishioners and Pastors are similar to a garden that needs sunlight.

Pastors you were present during many of my sacred occasions,
Such as baptisms, funerals, memorial services, and wedding celebrations,
You have called and visited the hospitals when we needed you,
It is refreshing to get one of your phone calls and hear you say, "I am praying for you,"
Pastors help Parishioners to continue.

Pastors do not give up on us and we will not give up on you,
Together as a faith community we will see one another through,
Keep your bible in hands, but more importantly on your tongue and in your heart,
Take care of yourself so you help take care of us from the start,
It will be difficult for you to be pastoral if you are torn apart.

A BAPTISM

Water centuries old that hovered over the earth while it was formless,
Water flooded the earth during the days of Noah,
Water parted the Red Sea for the Egyptians which was led by Moses,
Water that John the Baptist used to baptize Jesus Christ,
Water is an outward expression of inward grace,
Water falls from the heaven above and comes up from the earth below,
Water centuries old hovered over me while I was formless.

A FUNERAL

Feet that took their last step and lungs that took their last breath,
Eyes that shut for the last time and words that spoke their last rhyme,
Tears of sorrow, some family and friends not wanting to see tomorrow,
Without the person lying in a coffin still, or cremated to ashes,
Memories fluttering around in people's mind and they often remember the best,
Yet they are usually feeling their worst and emotionally distraught,
Attempting to acknowledge death while highlighting the eternity that follows.

HOSPITAL VISITS

Needles, patches, machines, medications, wheelchairs, rooms that are spacious and little,
Doctors, nurses, clean-up crews, and administrators walking through long hallways,
Can I get you a cup of water?
Do you want me to contact the nurse?
The weather is fine outside,
Life does resemble a baseball game that throws us fast and curve balls,
Yes, right now I can pray.

I intended to stay 15 minutes, but they insisted I stay 35,
Could have stayed 35 minutes, but they insisted that I stay only 5,
I can not find this hospital because I never visited this one before,
The traffic is terrible and I will try not to go in this direction during this time anymore,
Why do I feel, in this hospital, I am getting the grand tour?
We will trust God for tomorrow and thank God for today,
Yes, right now I can pray.

God guide my feet, behavior, and words,
Allow this interaction to be like a smooth melodious tune from a hummingbird,
Send your angels to meet me where the physically sick dwell,
Use me as an instrument to assist the weak, tired, and frail,
May my ears hear the words that need to be heard on this day,
Permit the words to be said that I need to say,
Yes, right now I can pray.

SUNDAY SCHOOL

Sunday School is the place where I first learned to read,
No matter how slow I read, or how much help I needed with the words,
it was alright,
I gave summaries of the Sunday School's lesson to the congregation
representing,
My class and the church positively affirmed my speeches,
They clapped when I stuttered without being able to stop, they clapped
when I did not, Even understand my own points that I was trying to
convey,
The congregation encouraged me to continue to learn and speak
without any delay,
That is where I first encountered teachers that believed in me, my
history, and my people, They believed in what they were saying,
Believed in righteousness and doing what is right.

Sunday School is where I learned that God created,
The heaven and the earth and on the seventh day God rested.
I learned that Moses was adopted like me and God used him,
To split the Red Sea for his people to be free,
I saw older students who articulated the bible and their relationship
to God,
That scene inspired me, excited me, and aroused me to read and learn,
and learn and read,
That is the place where I was first encouraged to give my tithe to God
through nickles, Dimes, quarters, and one dollar bills in the collection
plate,
I saw older men and women reading the bible, explaining some of the
mysteries,
They shared stories and testimonies of faith, hope, and mercy that
helped give me fuel to, Continue to live this Christian journey.

Sunday School was where I was taught that understanding the information was more Important than competing for a grade,
I learned to be quiet, keep still, mind my manners, and behave,
I was told that black was beautiful, beautiful was black,
Black and beautiful were in the Holy Bible,
My people are in the scriptures; the scriptures are in me,
Sunday School gave me homework to read the night before.
I remembered scripture verses, biblical stories, and more,
Sunday School is the foundation of my Christian education- it is the core.

SUNDAY SERMONS

Words turned into sentences etched from ancient scripture,
Sentences turned into paragraphs passed down to generations,
Paragraphs turned into proclamations to what was, is, and yet to be,
Proclamations turned into affirmations or convictions for ears,
People needing to hear messages that convey God cares.

Topics, titles, and three points that highlight spiritual truths,
Explanations and analysis with God being enough proof,
15, 30, 45, 60, and sometimes even 90 minutes long,
It can take place before, during and after gospel songs.
Praises going up, blessings coming down, which makes concerns and
worries gone.

The introduction, body, conclusion, all pointing ultimately to the
Christian Trinity,
Addressing a chaotic world trying to create more peace, love, and
harmony,
Compared to Jesus there is not a friend,
Sunday sermons refuel, refocus, reenergize again and again,
Glory, glory, glory, amen and amen.

CHAPTER TWO
LETTERS FROM A PASTOR'S DESK

"The greatest lesson a leader can teach is that life is a process, not an event."

— Johnetta B. Cole

SERVING GOD AND COUNTRY

(I wrote this article for the Orange Pages, the church's newsletter, while I served as full-time Associate Pastor at Orange United Methodist Church in Chapel Hill, NC in April 2003.)

I have received many questions and had stimulating conversations with many of you since my return from a tour of duty at Maxwell Air Force Base in Montgomery, Alabama, this past February. I am an Air Force Chaplain in the Reserves (Category B). Category B status means that I serve a minimum of four weeks a year, instead of serving a minimum one weekend a month (Category A status). Today, several American religious communities are debating topics such as a Christian's role in war, pacifism and patriotism. I write this article not to promote my personal views, but to share my past and current military experiences solicited by those of you in the congregation.

At times I am presented with the following question from colleagues and friends, "Kenny, why are you a Chaplain in the Air Force? How can you support the United States Military?" My quick response is usually, "In the midst of war, Christian ministry is needed most." I will now give you a longer answer. During my senior year at The Citadel, I was Third Battalion Religious Officer (Cadet Captain). I was spiritually responsible for 250 cadets and it was an awesome experience that will stay with me for many years. During that year, I conducted Bible studies, devotion and prayer services, preached in The Citadel Chapel (which I was invited to do again as a graduate), participated in a funeral at Arlington National Cemetery (a deceased Citadel graduate Air Force pilot), counseled and answered many questions concerning death, relationships, and Jesus Christ. It was during these experiences that the military chaplaincy bug bit me!

I entered the Air Force Chaplaincy Candidacy program during my first year at Duke Divinity School, which meant I spent the summers between academic semesters on a military base participating in chaplaincy training. One aspect of the military chaplaincy that I enjoy is the interaction with people from a variety of denominational religious, ethnic, vocation, and national backgrounds. I still seriously consider the idea of becoming an active duty Air Force Chaplain and I feel blessed to have that option. After graduating from Duke Divinity School, I received my commission as an Air Force Chaplain in the Reserves (Category B). The military chaplaincy defines its mission as "a visible reminder of the Holy." Military personnel have the constitutional right of freedom of religion. Therefore, military chaplains representing numerous denominations and religions are an essential component of military life. As an Air Force Chaplain, I preach, teach, counsel, perform weddings, conduct funerals, and perform many other duties that a civilian pastor performs, except I do it in a military uniform labeled United States Air Force.

We in the US are living during a peculiar moment in time. While this country stands as the most powerful in the world, our society has been exposed as vulnerable to violent domestic and international forces. I do not believe that America is synonymous with Christianity or that it is blameless regarding war, injustice and oppression. I believe that with all of its faults and mistakes, America is still the best country for people to have unparalleled opportunities and freedoms. Religiously and spiritually I serve God and my citizenship directs me to serve my country. America is my country and I intentionally choose to remain here and accept all our shortcomings. I am proud to work for my God and country simultaneously.

WHO IS MY NEIGHBOR?

(I wrote this article for the Orange Pages, the church's newsletter, while I served as full-time Associate Pastor at Orange United Methodist Church in Chapel Hill, NC in September 2002.)

A German theologian by the name of Dietrich Bonhoffer said, "If the church solely exists within the church it can no longer call itself the church." Unfortunately, Bonhoffer was imprisoned, and one of the last requests from Adolph Hitler was Bonhoffer's death by execution right before the end of World War II.

In 2002, we often find ourselves asking the question found in the gospel of Luke 10:29. In June, I had the privilege of giving a short devotional and offered communion to some of the residents of Shepherd House, an assisted living facility located 15 minutes away. I had an awesome experience with the residents on that Sunday afternoon.

I must include that Ms. Fay Daniel's presence and involvement made my first visit to the Shepherd House most reassuring. They welcomed me with smiles and handshakes. All of us talked, sang, laughed, and prayed together for almost 45 minutes. However, the experience will indeed stay with me much longer.

It pleases me to know that Orange UMC is scheduled on a monthly basis to visit places such as the homeless shelter (Inter Faith Council), prison (Orange Correctional Center), Shepherd House, and Chapel Hill Rehabilitation Center. I encourage all of you to participate in visiting the various places in which Orange UMC visits on a monthly basis.

Orange UMC has members at many of the noted facilities in the area. You would most definitely make a new friend. A personal prayer of mine is that I will someday receive visits when the time comes in my life that I can no longer travel on my own.

I know people are busy and sometimes just feel uncomfortable in certain settings. I surely did not know what to expect walking in the doors for the very first time of the Shepherd House. I do not know what to expect this September 1 at 7:30 p.m. when I walk through the doors of Orange Correctional Center. In spite of this, I reflect upon the words of Jesus' response to the question, "Who is my neighbor?"

THE HOLY GHOST IS HAUNTING ME AND WILL NOT LEAVE ME ALONE

(I wrote this article for the Orange Pages, the church's newsletter, while I served as full-time Associate Pastor at Orange United Methodist Church in Chapel Hill, NC in November 2002.)

October 31 has been a season when ghosts are celebrated in various ways. One year I was on a panel of speakers about the topic of Halloween, which later gave me fuel for a sermon that I preached a year or two later. Every October, I think of the question that was addressed to me almost five years ago pertaining to Christians and Halloween. A person asked me the following question: "Should a Christian believe or celebrate in supernatural activities such as ghosts?" I thought for a few seconds. Then I responded as follows:

Ghosts and supernatural activities are not anything new to Christians. In fact, Christians believe in God's Holy Spirit, which is also referred to as the Holy Ghost, especially for some of our Pentecostal brothers and sisters and a few other Christian circles. Furthermore, Christianity is based upon several supernatural activities and events such as: 1.) God dividing the Red Sea for Moses, 2.) Jesus' birth to Mary, and 3.) Jesus' resurrection from the grave- only to name a few.

Christians have always and still believe in God's miraculous power against reality or what human eyes can see. Christians do not worship or praise demonic existence yet we do acknowledge their presence in the world in which we live. Nevertheless, other Christians and I depend on the Holy Ghost or God's Holy Spirit to guide, protect, and keep us from hurt, harm, or danger.

In John 14:15-21, Jesus tells of the Holy Spirit not leaving his followers. I thank God for not being left alone in this world or to my own vices, the few I have. Therefore, it is a blessing that Christians are haunted on a daily basis. We see, celebrate, and praise God's activity and presence in the world at times when we are the only ones who are able to realize what's really going on.

MAKE ROOM FOR CHRISTMAS, LUKE 2:7

(I wrote this article for the Orange Pages, the church's newsletter, while I served as full-time Associate Pastor at Orange United Methodist Church in Chapel Hill, NC in December 2002.)

The Christmas Season is one of the most celebrated times of the year across the globe. On every continent, Jesus Christ's birth will get some type of recognition from a variety of unique cultures. In America, several stores will advertise Christmas sales for customers so that people can exchange gifts; television stations will broadcast Christmas shows; and radio stations will play Christmas songs across the airwaves.

Today, Christians find themselves in the midst of a society that is bombarded with commercialism that does not have anything to do with Jesus' birth. As Christians we should seriously think about whom we identify with during this Advent Season. Do we identify or follow the wise men traveling from afar searching for, wanting, and being in relationship with Jesus? Or do we identify with the inn or village not making any room for Jesus to come into our lives, because we are occupied with other people, places, or things?

Let us make room for Jesus Christ in our lives. I do enjoy Christmas parties, gifts, etc, but I do recognize that they have the ability to blur or eliminate the true meaning of the Christmas Season in my life. Join me in making room for Jesus Christ this Season. Are you available?

A DREAM UNFULFILLED

(I wrote this article for the Orange Pages, the church's newsletter, while I served as full-time Associate Pastor at Orange United Methodist Church in Chapel Hill, NC in January 2003.)

All across the United States of America and a few other countries the birthday of Rev. Dr. Martin Luther King, Jr. will be celebrated on the third Monday of January. King's birthday, January 15, 1929, is celebrated and remembered in several different ways. There are many events that King achieved during his life. King received his undergraduate education at Morehouse College and received a Ph. D. from Boston University. I am always in awe of the insight King illustrated in two of his five books entitled "Why We Can't Wait"-1963 and "The Strength To Love"- 1963. Many people will highlight King being a recipient of the coveted Nobel Peace Prize in 1964, walking in various marches, speaking eloquent speeches such as "I Have A Dream"- 1963 and writing letters such as the renowned "Letter from Birmingham Jail"- April 16, 1963. One of the many things that come to my mind about King is his dream.

Rev. Dr. William Willimon, Dean of Duke University Chapel, author of over 40 books, and named one of the Twelve Most Effective Preachers in the English Speaking World by an international survey conducted by Baylor University, is a personal friend/mentor of mine. As a student of Dr. Willimon, I fondly remember a statement he made during one of his thought provoking lectures,

"I know some of you are excited about being in the ministry and others of you have heard words of encouragement from various people about you needing to be in the ministry. But quite honestly some of you probably need to run away as fast as you can, because you do not have the courage and nerve it takes. You will not want to be a prophet and priest. When I read the Bible I look at people like Amos, Nathan, Jeremiah, and Paul, all of whom stood up against governments, presidents,

rulers, and popular opinion. That is why there are not too many people like Rev. Martin Luther King, Jr. and Dietrich Bonhoeffer. Most of you will not be able to endure, because you will want to make too many friends and want to travel the easy road or of least resistant."

King not only had a dream, but he had the courage to announce it, encourage it, and he dared to live it in a society that defied every notion of what his dream meant. The sin of many Christians is not their actions, but their inactivity. There comes a time when silence can be dangerous. Fortunately for us, King refused to keep quiet even when it was convenient or arguably smart.

King's short life of only 39 years spanned from January 15, 1929 to April 4, 1968 when racism roamed freely in public all across America, rather than camouflage or only in private conversations. It was on August 28, 1963, five years before his death, that King announced to the world his dream of racial equality on the steps of the Lincoln Memorial in Washington, D.C.,

"I have a dream my four little children will one day live in a nation where they will not be judged by the color of the skin but by the content of their character." (I Have Dream Speech, pg. 219, A Testament of Hope, The Essential Writings and Speeches of Martin Luther King, Jr. edited by James M. Washington)

King's dream was heard in America during a time when segregation had its venomous hands around America and killed anyone or thing that rebelled against its sinister laws. Today, people of various ethnic groups are going to schools and places of work together; we should not forget that the U.S. Government had to legally enforce it against cruel resistance. Fortunately, the venomous hands of segregation have weakened, and it does not divide people in America as much as it did in the past. However, America still has a lot of progress yet to be made. Unfortunately, religious organizations, such as churches, have and still are moving slowly behind the secular organizations such as schools and places of work in race relations. Christians should set the model for true Christian fellowship for the whole world to see.

I write this article to both commend and challenge Orange United Methodist Church as we acknowledge Rev. Dr. Martin Luther King, Jr.'s birthday in the year 2003. I commend Orange Church for actively participating in becoming a reflection of the body of our Lord and Savior Jesus Christ. It is unmistakably difficult to achieve King's dream in America since historically the citizens have systematically been taught to disassociate by the color of one's skin. While confined inside an Alabama jail cell, King wrote,

> *"In deep disappointment, I have wept over the laxity of the church. But be assured that my tears have been tears of love. There can be no deep disappointment where there is not love. Yes, I love the church; I love her sacred walls. How could I do otherwise? I am in the rather unique position of being the son, the grandson and the great-grandson of preachers. Yes, I see the church as the body of Christ. But, oh! How we have blemished and scarred that body through social neglect and fear of being nonconformists.*

> *There was a time when the church was very powerful. It was during that period when the early Christians rejoiced when they were deemed worthy to suffer for what they believed. In those days the church was not merely a thermometer that recorded the ideas and principles of popular opinion; it was a thermostat that transformed the mores of society. Wherever the early Christians entered a town the power structure got disturbed and immediately sought to convict them for being "disturbers of the peace" and "outside agitators." But they went on with the conviction that they were "a colony of heaven," and had to obey God rather than man. They were small in number but big in commitment. They were too God-intoxicated to be "astronomically intimidated." They brought an end to such ancient evils as infanticide and gladiatorial contest."* (Letter From Birmingham City Jail, pgs.299-300, A

Testament of Hope, The Essential Writings and Speeches of
Martin Luther King, Jr. edited by James M. Washington)

There are strides taking place in America, but too often the waves of
racial progress do not reach millions of people who find themselves
on a desolate, lonely island of life labeled exclusively for only African
Americans, Asians, Caucasians, Spanish, etc. Ironically, interracial
congregations are more challenging to develop than assigning a pastor
to a cross-racial appointment. I challenge Orange Church to continue
to intentionally advance toward racial unity, and avoid the tempting
pitfall of complacency or erroneous gradualism. Even in 2003 it
continues to take great courage to fulfill King's dream.

I will now share a personal story with you, because I realize that our
time together will come to an end soon. I must admit that it took
courage for me to become Associate Pastor of Orange Church when
I graduated from Duke University Divinity School. Upon graduation
I was offered a few other employment opportunities in cross-racial
appointments in and outside of North Carolina. I will make an honest
confession to you that one of the major contributing factors why I did
not accept the other cross-racial opportunities was because I would
have been the first person of color on the Pastoral staff. My refusal
may surprise a few, but racism stills exists in our society whether
subtle or overt. I knew through personal observation and experience
that racism runs as deep and long within American culture as the
Mississippi River. At the time, I did not want to travel down that
path immediately after my divinity graduation and more importantly
I wanted to protect Michelle from the agony of ignorant attitudes and
beliefs. One can argue that I based my decision on lack of courage and
faith. Or one can argue that I based my decision on sheer logic. Some
of my family, friends, colleagues, and peers shared genuine sentiments
of concern for my decision to join Orange Church's staff. I concluded
that my ministry paralleled the words of King,

*"Just as the eighth century prophets left their little villages and
carried their thus saith the Lord" far beyond the boundaries
of their hometowns; and just as the Apostle Paul left his little
village of Tarsus and carried the gospel of Jesus Christ to*

practically every hamlet and city of the Graeco-Roman world, I too am compelled to carry the gospel of freedom beyond my particular hometown." (Letter From Birmingham City Jail, pg. 291, A Testament of Hope, The Essential Writings and Speeches of Martin Luther King, Jr. edited by James M. Washington)

At any rate, an attractive component and one of the main reasons I decided to serve at Orange Church was that it had a good track record with a Pastoral cross-racial appointment and interracial parishioners. Even with these positive attributes, I still acknowledged the ill race conditions of the larger society in which Orange Church resides.

In order for all of us to fulfill King's dream we must be Christian enough to go through growing pains. It is sometimes painful to experience and realize that the world does not usually march to the tune of God's word. God's tune is usually counterculture. The culture will tell you cross-racial appointments can not or should not occur. The culture will convey the message that interracial congregations are unsuccessful or useless. God's tune sends a different message because it is a message of love, peace, and unity embracing diversity for all of God's people. I believe and am happy to know that Orange Church is working toward turning King's dream into reality. It is not always easy nor is it always fun, therefore like all relationships it takes work. Until all of us continue to deliberately work in all areas of life to promote racial unity- King's dream will be *a dream unfulfilled.*

LOVE GOD FIRST

(I wrote this article for the Orange Pages, the church's newsletter, while I served as full-time Associate Pastor at Orange United Methodist Church in Chapel Hill, NC in February 2003.)

February 14 is Valentine's Day, Happy Valentine's Day to one and all! The following are three major reasons why I always look forward to the month of February: 1.) My Birthday is February 25; and this year I will turn 26 years old; 2.) February is highlighted as Black History Month, and 3.) Valentines' Day is celebrated. In this article I will elaborate on the latter, being Valentine's Day.

Think about when you were in grade school and you thought you were in love. Some of you wrote letters that consisted of the following instructions: "Do you love me? *Yes* or *No*. Circle *yes* or *no*. Please circle *yes*." When you became old enough to use the telephone, some of you stayed on the phone all day and all night. Then finally you got to drive and go on an official date unsupervised. God have mercy upon us all! It is a nice feeling to be loved by someone, because everybody likes positive attention. It is also good to love somebody, no matter if it is your sweetheart, your brother, your sister, your mother, or father. However, we should not allow any relationship to interfere with the love we have for God. Do not permit anyone or anything to come between you and God. Love God first!

Enjoy Valentine's Day, but also remember that flowers, candy, and nice restaurants still do not compare to the love that we receive from God. Please know that I hope you take February 14th to show someone special to you how much you appreciate and love him or her. Loving God first allows you to love other people, places, and things properly. You do not have to only share thoughtful sentiments during the month of February—do it as much as possible!

Who is the historical Valentine? The Catholic Church recognizes at least three different saints named Valentine or Valentinus. Saint Valentine is believed to have been a priest. The three most popular legends of this widely celebrated priest in Rome around 265 AD are as follows: 1.) Valentine continued to defy the law by performing illegal marriages for male soldiers to young ladies, 2.) Valentine helped Christians escape cruel Roman persecution, and 3.) Valentine may have written the first "Valentine" greeting himself (example: "From your Valentine") while in prison for refusing to stop Christian ministry to a young lady with whom he fell in love. At any rate, Valentine's life ended tragically because he attempted to do God's work until the final days of his human life.

Saint Valentine loved God first regardless of the consequences. Therefore, it brings new meaning to the following question that I will ask you in Christian love: "Will you be my Valentine?"

MEMORIES OF ORANGE UNITED METHODIST CHURCH, 1 CORINTHIANS 16:24

(I wrote this article for the church's newsletter as fulltime Associate Pastor at Orange United Methodist Church in Chapel Hill, NC in May 2003.)

This is the last article I will write for the Orange Pages; my last sermon will be May 25, 2003 and my last day of work as the full-time Associate Pastor of Orange UMC will be on May 30, 2003. First of all, Michelle and I thank all of you who have welcomed us into your church family through not merely words but most importantly through your actions. Orange UMC will always have a special place in my heart and I take with me fond memories. How could I not? We spent only a year together, but we have participated in some of life's most sacred events in unison. Some memories will include the following: We have worshiped God, praised God, prayed to God, thanked God, and brought concerns to God together as a congregation. We have spent time in hospital rooms during periods of sickness, operations, and the birth of a baby. We have shared special moments in the church's sanctuary for weddings, funerals, baptisms, New Year's Eve, Sunday morning worship, Bible studies (Disciple I and Lenten Devotionals) and communion services. We shook hands, held hands, hugged, kissed, wept, and laughed together in times of disappointment, fear, and joy.

This year has been full of activity. We have played basketball, flown together in airplanes, eaten at restaurants, eaten at your home, and eaten at my home together. We have told jokes, secrets, and stories from the past, and hopes for the future. We have learned, taught, listened, talked, agreed, disagreed and at times had different opinions. We ate breakfast, lunch, dinner, and sometimes a snack in between. We have communicated face-to-face, by email, by telephone, and by letter. We have fellowshipped in the rain, sunshine, snow, heat and all types of weather. To put it simply, we have traveled together on this journey called life.

It has been an honor and privilege for me to be your Pastor. I have enjoyed working with the other Pastors and staff at Orange UMC and I am confident that they will continue to lead you in the right direction. My next appointment will be at Hope UMC (www.hopeumc.org) in Southfield, Michigan, as fulltime Associate Pastor starting July 1st. I am excited to move into a new church community, but I will have fond memories of Orange UMC and the Raleigh-Durham-Chapel Hill area. I look forward to working with Hope UMC's prominent Senior Pastor Rev. Dr. Carlyle F. Stewart III, who has authored 10 books and counting.

Take care, take God, and 2 Corinthians 13-14.

ECUMENICAL MINISTRY AND
INTERRELIGIOUS DIALOGUE

(I wrote this response paper after studying in Rome, Italy during the summer of 2004)

The world is becoming smaller every day. In America, a growing number of Elementary, Middle and High schools, Colleges, and Universities are becoming a reflection of the United Nations. Visiting a local grocery store or mall in many communities is an interreligous event. People from different religions and faith traditions are working together, marrying one another, and living in the same neighborhoods in a faster rate than ever before in American history and throughout the world. While studying in Rome, Italy at the Centro Pro Unione, the instructors and students explored the following questions in which this paper will address: What were some of the transitions that the ecumenical and interreligious movement went through from past to present? Has the transition been smooth or tumultuous? What directions are the ecumenical and interreligious movements going in now?

I am an African-American United Methodist Pastor and United States Air Force Chaplain Reservist serving in the Detroit Annual Conference, which is located in Southeast Michigan. I have noticed that many local communities across the United States of America are becoming just as diverse as the military. For example, a common scene in any of the affluent suburbs outside of the city of Detroit would display a Protestant jogging on the sidewalk, passing by a Muslim owned and operated store, which is located less than a block from a Catholic Church that is across the street from a Lutheran Church. I believe there are several ecumenical and interreligious events all around us and it begs the following question, "How did we get to this point religiously in our lives as a global community?"

The biblical foundations for ecumenical and interreligious movements are located in the Bible from Genesis to Revelation. Therefore,

ecumenical and interreligious movements were not created in the
21st century. The Old Testament informs us that some people chose
to follow other gods instead of Elohim Adoni. The book of Exodus
notes the following,

> **"When the people saw that Moses was so long in coming
> down from the mountain, they gathered around Aaron
> and said, "Come, make us gods who will go before us. As
> for this fellow Moses who brought us up out of Egypt, we
> don't know what has happened to him." (Exodus 32:1,
> NIV)**

Furthermore, the New Testament highlights disagreements within
various Christian faith communities that did not always require a
person to get expelled. For example, the Gospel of John notes the
following scripture by illustrating Thomas disagreeing with the other
disciples,

> **"...Unless I see the nail marks in his hands and put my
> finger where the nails were, and put my hand into his
> side, I will not believe it." (John 20:25, NIV)**

> **"A week later [Jesus'] disciples were in the house again,
> and Thomas with them..." (John 20:26, NIV)**

It is important to know our ecumenical and interreligious past so we
will have an idea of where we have been and a sense of where we want
to go.

Ecumenical and Interreligious movements partly stem from difference
of beliefs and opinions.   Not only did Jesus' twelve disciples not
always agree with one another but sometimes they disagreed with
Jesus. When Jesus fed the five thousand people some of his disciples
did not agree with the methods he used. The Gospel of John notes
a few disciples wanting to go contrary to Jesus' plans stating the
following,

"Philip answered him, "Eight months' wages would not
buy enough bread for each one to have a bite!" (John 6:7,
NIV)

"Another of his disciples, Andrew, Simon Peter's brother,
spoke up, "Here is a boy with five small barley loaves and
two small fish, but how far will they go among so many?"
(John 6:8-9, NIV)

I believe it is important to look at ecumenical and interreligious
movements as a natural way of life that began in the biblical days,
continues today, and will most assuredly move forward in the future.

Another topic we explored the first week of study in Rome, Italy was
Eastern Christianity, sometimes referred to as the "Eastern Orthodox
Church". This topic highlights the importance of the accuracy in labels
or language within religious communities. I realized that the "Eastern
Orthodox Church" is not just one church, there are many Orthodox
Churches in the East. Furthermore, Orthodox Churches exist all over
the globe. Much like the Southern Baptist Church exists not only in
the Southern geographical regions of the United States of America,
but also exists in the North, West, and internationally. The Eastern
Orthodox Church exists not only in the east but also in other regions of
the globe. Furthermore, entirely different sects of Orthodox Churches
exist with little to no relationship with the Eastern Orthodox Church.

The instructors emphasized that the "Catholic Church" should not
be assumed or implied as the "Roman Catholic Church", because
there are several other "Catholic Churches". Precise language and
labels helps to respect diverse individuals that live in ecumenical
and interreligious communities. Precise language helps prevent faith
traditions from being ignored or insulted in the world in which we
live. For example, as a United Methodist Pastor it is essential that I
mention "United" before "Methodist" as oppose to just "Methodist"
as if African-Methodists, Southern Methodists, Wesleyan Methodists,
and other Methodist do not exist or are not significant. My Mom
always used to tell me to "watch your mouth", meaning be conscious
and thoughtful of the words I would speak. Communities of faith also

need to "watch their mouths" in order that we all may live together in peace, love, and harmony.

From a Roman Catholic Perspective, one of the major moments in religious history that began the continuation of the ecumenical movement within Christianity was the Protestant Reformation, which was greatly influenced by Martin Luther. Martin Luther who was once a Catholic professor decided that he could no longer be silent about the abuses that he felt within the hierarchy of Catholicism. Luther also felt that the Catholic Church Councils were ineffective and elitist. David C. Steinmetz notes,

> "....Luther attempted to define more narrowly the nature and task of a council. After a lengthy discussion in which he scrutinized the records of the councils of Jerusalem, Nicaea, Constantinople, Ephesus, and Chalcedon, he concluded that a council could not, and had never been expected to, establish new articles of belief beyond the articles contained in Holy Scripture. Councils defend and explain teaching which the prophets and apostles have already articulated. Therefore, there is nothing valid in the teaching of a council which is not first and more powerfully stated in Scripture itself. A council, then, "is nothing but a consistory, a royal court, a supreme court or the like, in which the judges, after hearing the parties, pronounce sentence, but with this humility, 'For the sake of the law'. (*Luther in Context*, pg. 89)

Many people left the Catholic Church to follow Luther's lead that would later help create up Lutheran Church in addition to igniting other Christian denominations. Some people followed other leaders of the Protestant Reformation such as John Calvin and Ulrich Zwingli. Later in history countless other reformations would occur to assist in the creation of well over 100 Christian denominations. Depending on who you are, fortunately or unfortunately, more Christian denominations are still being created today.

How do all theses Christian denominations interact with one another other than passing by one another churches to get to their own?

Well, numerous churches participate in and assist the World Council of Churches. One of the World Council of Churches' objectives is for the various denominations to better understand one another and work together in common Christian missions. The World Council of Churches is a good vehicle to help bring into being healthy ecumenical communities. It is nearly impossible for faith communities to get to know one another if there is no communication. Communication helps eliminate negative stereotypes and prejudices that can easily arise if there is no truthful or intentional socialization.

What are some of the causes that prevent Christian denominations from communicating with one another? What are some of the causes that prevent religions from communicating with one another? One of the components that prevent some Christian denominations from communicating with one another is turbulent past experiences that were never addressed or resolved. Some religions also have painful or violent histories toward one another, which can possibly hinder reconciliation or move forward to mutual respect and collaboration. A lot of Christian denominations are threatening to split because of different opinions pertaining to clergy sexuality and same sex marriage. It is ludicrous to think that all Christians or religions will ever agree on every theological issue on this side of creation, however it is a realistic and noble goal for all religious persons to treat one another with respect, dignity, and civility.

As a clergyperson, I personally feel somewhat responsible for educating and promoting peace between all devout followers. I believe all devout leaders such as religious teachers and clergy people ought to speak in an intelligent manner to their congregations while being conscious that their words have the possibility to provoke actions. It is destructive for a society or societies to have followers of religions fearful of one another. Kevin Phillips wrote the following in *The Christian Century*,

"To not a few Religious Right leaders, Islam itself is essentially evil. Jerry Falwell called the Prophet Muhammad a "terrorist", but later apologized. Pat Robertson called him a "wild-eyed fanatic", a "robber" and a "brigand".

Franklin Graham, son of Billy, branded Islam "evil". Former Southern Baptist Convention President Jerry Vines called Muhammad a "demon-possessed pedophile". Press reports blamed Falwell's remarks for the gains by pro-al Qaeda radical parties in Pakistan's early 2003 provincial elections. Overall, post invasion international surveys published by the Washington-based Pew Center reported that in countries from North Africa through the Middle East to Indonesia, Muslim regard for the United States had plummeted; in many nations, respondents preferred Osama bin Laden to George W. Bush." (July 13, 2004, pg. 9)

Religious leaders should not degrade religions or religious figures with blanket negative statements without any extensive evidence. Furthermore, evidence should be given with the notion that it is opinionated and open to interpretation. Interreligious Dialogue and Ecumenical Ministries can not exist successfully when religious leaders denounce other religious leaders, figures and/or religions as "evil".

ECUMENICAL & INTERRELIGIOUS MOVEMENTS

The Roman Catholic Church created official ecumenical documents to help guide its large global membership to dwell in the midst of a growing ecumenical and interreligious world. The numerous Roman Catholic Church documents on ecumenical and interreligious affairs are suggestive, binding, and statutory allowing the method to be a work in progress. Knowing that religion is sensitive area of people's lives and to encourage and instruct people of different faiths to socialize, work, and worship together will probably not happen instantly. During the second week in Rome, Italy at the Centro Pro Unione we explored some the various ways the Roman Catholic Church and other Christian Churches officially engage in various ecumenical and interreligious dialogue and activities.

Religious people like words. We joyfully read words in the Bible; we anxiously hear words during worship services, and some Preachers pray and ask God for a "word" before they preach to name a few. Words make up a major component of what we do and who we are. It is insightful that the Roman Catholic Church and several other mainline denominations not only spoke words of religious unity but also wrote words to help congregations follow not only by words of speech, but also words on paper.

Two of the many documents that the Roman Catholic Church helped produced to promote unity amongst faith communities are *"Principles for guiding the search for Unity between the Catholic Church and the Coptic Orthodox Church and the protocol joint to the Principles"* (June 23, 1979) and *"Common Christological Declaration"* (signed in 1994 by Pope John Paul II and Patriarch Mar Dinkha IV of the Assyrian Church of the East). Two of the several documents that were produced from Christian mainline denominations promoting unity and collaboration between faith communities are *"Churches Uniting in Christ; A resource booklet for CUIC Congregations"* (edited by the Presbyterian Church U.S.A), and *"Called to be Neighbors & Witnesses: Guidelines for Interreligious Relationships"* (United Methodist Church, 2000). It is essential that Clergy and Parishioner alike can read what, where, and how their faith community and others are building bridges together.

Official documents from the various faith communities possess powerful statements. The Presbyterian USA's document *"Churches Uniting in Christ; A resource booklet for CUIC Congregations"* highlights 2 of the 8 marks of churches uniting Jesus Christ on page 2 by declaring the following,

> **"4. Provision for celebration of the Eucharist together with intentional regularity. This recognizes that the sacrament is at the heart of the church's life. Shared celebration of the Lord's Supper is a sign of unity in Christ. As Christians gather in all their diversity at on Table of the Lord, they give evidence that their communion is with Christ, and that they are in communion with one another in Christ. When Christians are unable or unwilling to partake together of the one Eucharist, they witness against themselves and**

give a visible demonstration of the brokenness of Christ's
body and the human community."

"5. Engagement together in Christ's mission on a regular
and intentional basis, especially a shared mission to
combat racism. The church engages in Christ's mission
through worship, proclamation of the gospel, evangelism,
education and action that embodies God's justice, peace
and love. The commitment made by the members of
Churches Uniting in Christ includes all of these, so that
hearts and minds may be changed. The participating
churches will also recognize, however, a particular and
emphatic call to "erase racism" by challenging the system
of white privilege that has so distorted life in this society
and in the churches themselves. Indeed, this call is a
hallmark of the new relationship."

The Presbyterian Church U.S.A. is encouraging and joining the
universal Christian Church to eliminate racism, this is contributing
factor that creates new denominations and separate physical church
buildings side by side within the same denomination. On pages 1 - 2
in the United Methodist Church's document entitled *"Called to be
Neighbors & Witnesses: Guidelines for Interreligious Relationships"*
(2000) notes the following,

"The emergence of religiously diverse societies and
the new dynamics in old religious communities have
prompted many faith communities to reconsider how they
relate to one another and to prevailing secular ideologies.
This represents a great opportunity for learning and an
enhanced understanding of our common concerns. Yet,
there is also danger that religious tensions will lead to
oppression of religious minorities and curtailment of
religious freedom with real potential for armed conflict.
At a time when worldwide problems of human suffering
due to poverty, wars, and political oppression are so
vast and pervasive that no one faith can solve them,
tensions between religious groups often prevent the level

of cooperation needed to respond more adequately. As ancient religions demonstrate new life and power to speak to the deepest human concerns, Christians are pressed toward a deeper understanding of other faith traditions and a reexamination of their own claims to a global mission to all people."

The United Methodist Church is acknowledging the power and strength of different religions intentionally in fellowship together for the betterment of the world. On page 3 the document highlights the following,

"Today, our Lord's call to neighborliness (Luke 10:27) includes the "strangers" of other faith traditions who live in our towns and cities. It is not just that historical events have forced us together. Christianity itself impels us to love our neighbors and to seek to live in contact and mutually beneficial relationships, in community, with them."

How many Clergy and Parishioners actually read or desire to read ecumenical and interreligious literature? How many Clergy and Parishioners actually attempt to implement some of the suggestions and instructions into their own life and church to promote an ecumenical and interreligious friendly atmosphere? Some churches have implemented intentional ecumenical services for around 2 to 3 times a year, which usually consist of a combination of Christmas, Easter, Good Friday, and New Year worship services. Some churches have implemented intentional interreligious services that usually consist of a combination of the World Day of Peace service and remembrance of September 11, 2001 service. It is important for Clergy and Parishioners to use the ecumenical and interreligious literature that is available.

The concept of "receptivity" was also explored in the second week of study at the Centre Pro Unione. Webster's Dictionary defines the word "receptivity" as **having the quality of receiving, taking in, or admitting and/or able or quick to receive knowledge, ideas, etc.** The instructors defined "religious receptivity" as "something that is offered and taken simultaneously." Why is reception an important component in interreligious dialogue and ecumenical affairs? Why must something be offered? Why must something be taken? As language is important as noted earlier, so is receptivity amongst religious practices with Christian traditions in order to have a substantial amount of unity.

Receptivity has taken place in more denominations than others are. For example, most Mainline Protestant Churches such as Methodist, Presbyterian, and some Lutheran are receptive to sharing Holy Communion together. These mainline protestant churches intentionally decided to become unified at the Lords' Table. Meaning, they are receptive to receive and offer Holy Communion to a denomination not their own. This particular receptivity around the Lord's Table helps create more religious dialogue and unity. Another common area of receptivity amongst the previously noted Mainline Protestant Churches is the act of performing a wedding ceremony. Meaning, mostly all clergy from the Mainline Protestant Denominations can perform a wedding ceremony for another's' parishioners.

Receptivity allows opportunities for interreligious and ecumenical communities to worship, praise, attend, and participate in religious events more often than not. The Catholic Church does not have as much receptivity as it relates to Holy Communion and wedding ceremonies. The Catholic Church's official stance on Holy Communion is that Catholics are not allowed to receive communion from a non-Catholic Clergy person and a non-Catholic parishioner is not supposed to take Holy Communion from a Catholic. Catholic parishioners are officially supposed to get married by a Catholic priest even in the case the person they are marrying is not a Catholic. Therefore, the Catholic Church's non-receptivity in Holy Communion and wedding ceremonies does not allow Catholics and non-Catholics to unite at the Lord's Table nor does it allow them to fully participate at wedding ceremonies.

Different religions typically participate more in "national, special, civil" worship services such as Thanksgiving and New Year's Day rather than "biblical, historical, or spiritual" worship services Christmas and Easter. For example, a lot of September 11 religious worship services include a variety of religions such as Christian,

Muslim, Jewish, Buddhist, and Hindu clergy or other representatives. However, it would be highly unlikely for Muslims and most Jews to celebrate or participate in an Easter worship service. To maintain a sense of unity among different religious groups it is good for Clergy and Parishioners alike to promote, attend, and encourage one another to share in ministry.

When receptivity is not shared among religious or Christian denominations it leaves a group feeling less than, cheated, or ignored. It is essential for all faith groups to have parameters during interreligious and ecumenical affairs so that the probability of a faith community's being ignored is alleviated rather than intensified. John Cogley, William B. Greenspun, and William Norgren noted the "Ten Commandments for the Ecumenical Age" in the following,

1. **Remember that saints and sinners are to be found in all branches of Christianity.**
2. **Do not look to conversion as the proper result of ecumenism.**
3. **Do not attempt to achieve charity at the expense of truth.**
4. **Do not attempt to serve truth at the expense of charity.**
5. **Do not question another's sincerity or lightly impute superstition, ignorance or fear in order to explain why they believe as they do.**
6. **Respect what others deem holy.**
7. **Do not defend the indefensible.**
8. **Work together for the common good, as citizens equal before the law.**
9. **Pray together.**
10. **Leave theology to the theologians.**
    (*Living Room Dialogues*, **New York/Glen Rock; NJ: National Council of Christians Churches/ Paulist Press, 1965, pp.43-56)**

The *Ten Commandments for the Ecumenical Age* is worth promoting when engaging in interreligious and ecumenical affairs because faith communities are definitely interacting with another. What's more, people within the same religious group often think and act somewhat different within their own faith community.

It is wise for faith communities to officially publish sound ecumenical and interreligious literature so people will be able to not rely on gossip, heresy, myths, or prejudices toward other faith communities. Some churches are intentionally creating ecumenical pastoral teams. I am currently employed as an Associate Pastor at Hope United Methodist Church where United Methodists, African Methodists, and Baptist Clergy Persons help make up the Pastoral Team. We are able to minister to the well over 3,000-member congregation in ways I would have never thought of because of the ecumenical dimension. Many of the various clergy of Hope UMC representing different Christian sects are able to relate to the members with various faith backgrounds.

There is value when Mainline Churches implement ecumenical components within their congregations and to not leave it solely for Nondenominational Churches. At the very least, Churches ought to have pulpit exchanges, choir exchanges, and religious or holiday services together throughout the year. If more members of churches, mosques, and synagogues see their pastors, rabbis, and imams participate in interreligous and ecumenical activities it would have an enormous effect in a positive way. People usually follow their respected leaders and church people are no exception.

ECUMENICAL & INTERRELIGIOUS MOVEMENTS

Models of division and models of unity were explored during week three in Rome, Italy at the Centro Pro Unione. To effectively talk about "models of unity", first we had to review "models of division". All groups, religious groups included, are not divided without reason. In fact, there are a variety of reasons, both big and small why groups of people are divided. Sometimes the unwritten rules can be just as effective if not more as the written rule. It is important to identify models of division and models of unity to understand the best method of operation in different interreligious and ecumenical affairs. Methods of operations for models of unity will vary according to contributing factors such as Christian denominations, world religions, and geographical region to name a few.

One major model of division is "inherited division". Inherited Theological or Cultural Divisions generally means that the particular division has been passed down religiously from one generation to the next by behavior, speech, and traditional behavior. Any type of inherited division can be challenging to identify because it is not written on any official documents or unofficial documents. You typically do not read inherited divisions; instead it is all the more laborious to identify the divisive wall. Inherited division is typically one of the easiest divisions for a faith community to continue because it was generally, personally, directly or indirectly taught how to build and maintain walls of division between them and other faith groups.

Another model of division that was identified at the Centre Pro Unione was theological division. Theological divisions are typically easier to find than most, because they are usually written on a document that can be found somewhere displayed in a place of worship, in a library book, on a pamphlet, and/or often publicly communicated by speech. We need civil unity amongst our religious communities in order to set a positive example for a secular world. The early Christian Church encouraged followers of Jesus Christa to promote peace. Ephesians notes the following,

"For Christ himself has brought us peace by making Jews and Gentiles one people. With his own body he broke down the wall that separated them and kept them enemies. He abolished the Jewish Law with its commandments and rules, in order to create out of the two races one new people in union with himself, in this way making peace. By his death on the cross Christ destroyed their enmity; by means of the cross he united both races into one body and brought them back to God. So Christ came and preached the Good News of peace to all- to you Gentiles, who were far away from God, and to the Jews, who were near to him. It is through Christ that all of us, Jews and Gentiles,

are able to come in the one Spirit into the presence of the Father." (2:14-18, Good News Translation)

Theological divisions usually require a group of theologians for a theological standpoint to change. However, theological divisions usually change faster and more often than the previously noted inherited cultural divisions.

For example, women were once restricted and could not hold the office of "pastor" in many of the Christian Mainline Denominations. There were theological stances that prohibited women to the pastoral office, but many denominations changed their policies with time. Theologians and parishioners began to interpret God's activity with the world and the Holy Bible with different interpretations that not only allowed, but also encouraged women to join their male counterparts in the pastorate. Theological divisions and cultural divisions in religious life are both complex and many variables help determine the outcome of how a faith community will worship and praise God.

Theological unity can allow different faiths to share in religious services. For example, various Christian faiths share communion together. The two particular faiths may not agree on every issue, but their agreement on the "Lords Table" enables them to break bread and drink wine in remembrance of Jesus' death so that we all may have eternal life. Another religious service that sometimes functions as an ecumenical event for Clergy to participate in is the wedding ceremony. The two Clergy representing two different faith communities may not agree on everything, but they agree on the issue pertaining to "wedding" in order to unite two people in holy matrimony.

A model of unity that we explored was "unity of work and mission". Unity of work and mission is when groups of people from different religions and Christian denominations work together toward a common goal. Unity of work and mission unites different religions that can possibly share in ministry for the homeless, hungry, and/or disenfranchised in our local community and world. Geographical location is also factor of division within religion. One geographical location can sometimes think that they have a monopoly of a particular faith that makes it challenging for two different national citizens to worship in harmony in the same church. Dale T. Irvin wrote the following in *The Christian Century,*

> **"Now, at the end of the modern age, the success of that missionary project (and especially of the apprehension of the gospel along the indigenous side of the line between missionary and convert) emerges as perhaps the most important factor in world Christian life today. Coupled with the staggering de-Christianization of the traditional European "homeland" of Christendom, the shift is enormous. Christianity, long identified as primarily a Western, European religion, is so no longer. It is now predominantly a religion of Africans, Asians and Latin Americans, and of the descendants of these regions who now live in the North Atlantic world. According to recent estimates, as many as 60 percent of the world's Christians now live in the Southern Hemisphere." (July 27, 2004, pg. 28)**

It is difficult for any country to lay claim that all of their citizens willingly profess one religion. A variety of religions are found everywhere and the tide is changing numerically across the globe for most faith communities and countries including Christianity and America which can no longer be thought of simultaneously.

In this election year of 2004, I have witnessed a new model of unity among religious communities pertaining to politics. Whoever said politics and religion does not mix? Is it truly a separation of church and state? Do Christians really want a separation of Church and State in America? While studying in Rome, it appeared that the Roman Catholic Church had an unmistakably element of control in Rome and the surrounding areas despite a surprising growing Muslim population, a growing Protestant population, and a stable Jewish population. If truth be told, the Roman Catholic Church has an element of power all throughout the world with national figures constantly seeking advice or approval from the Roman Catholic Pope. However, in this American election year of 2004, I have seen various religious groups representing a several religions and numerous Christian faiths working together to get a person elected to the United States Presidency and other offices around the country.

It is great to see religious groups come together to help make the United States of America and any other country a better place to live for all of its citizens. Too many religious communities have violent pasts with one another that make it difficult for sincere fellowship. The Catholics and Protestants have a turbulent past that involves murder, harsh estrangement, and war. Baptists, United Methodists, and Quakers have all crossed one another's path in history in ways that were not warm or hospitable. Christians, Muslims and Jews all have bloody histories filled with violence amongst one another which has harbored a lack of trust, fear, and hate. I hope that religious groups will be able to continue to move forward in a positive direction working together for a better tomorrow. The Centro Pro Unione taught us that in order for religious communities to effectively move forward they need to address any unjust past events responsibly. First of all, both sides must have an opportunity to *tell their story* and share their feelings pertaining to what took place and the affects. Faith communities must be attentive to other faith communities when tragic historic events have taken place in order to look ahead to a bright harmonious future.

It is important for the projected victim and oppressor to tell their story about a historic event in order for both parties to live comfortably in the present, but there are more steps that should take place for the *healing of memory*. The next step in religious reconciliation is the *purification of the past* between religions. Purification of past consists of ensuring that *the truth is told* after stories are told. Truth has a way of getting distorted, ignored, and confused over long periods of time. Purification of the past is essential particularly when books, movies and other media outlets help to support false information about historic events. The last, but not least step, is repentance in the fact of the harm done and not harming the party again and working toward genuine reconciliation. Repentance may include a change in attitude, behavior, and/or lifestyle. When someone asked Peter, one of Jesus' Disciples, for spiritual advice, Peter gave the following response "... **Repent and be baptized, every one of you, in the name of Jesus**

Christ for the forgiveness of your sins…" (Acts 2:38). Repentance is not easy, yet it is vital to help ensure that our future will not repeat our errors in the past.

My time spent in Rome, Italy gave me a much clearer picture and understanding of the Roman Catholic Church. While studying at the Centro Pro Unione I began to understand better the authority of The Pope and the profundity of the Roman Catholic Church structure. Peter Williams wrote the following about The Pope's role in the Roman Catholic Church,

> **"However, it also maintains that Scripture can be interpreted properly only through the magisterium, or teaching authority, of the institutional church. The fullness of this authority resides in the Papacy, which is the custodian of the body of teaching known as *Tradition*. Tradition is based on revelation as contained in Scripture, but also includes doctrines, such as the bodily assumption of the Virgin Mary into heaven. These are not explicit in Scripture but have been developed within the Catholic community over the centuries from implicit scriptural evidence. The Pope is further able to make infallible pronouncements on matters of faith and morals when he speaks *ex cathedra*- that is, officially from his "chair", which is a symbol of his office." (America's Religions: Traditions & Cultures, pg. 45)**

The Roman Catholic Church's structure was eye opening for a variety of reasons. First of all, I did not think any religious leader had that much authority over any church organization in the 21st Century. Second of all, some of my friends and a few family members are Roman Catholic and I never had any discussions on the authority of the Pope and the intricacies of the church structure. Last but not least, the educational experience has taught me to not assume or take anything for granted. To learn and understand, one should ask questions, investigate, and explore.

Visiting the Jewish Synagogue and Islamic Mosques were definitely a highlight of my educational experience in Rome. I am always delighted to talk to Jews and Muslims and my wife and I have personal close friends representing those religions among other faith communities. However, it was interesting to hear what the Jews and Muslims had to say in the shadow of Rome's Vatican City. It is amazing how religious people find it much easier to love God and not God's creation, which is a command of God.

The Centro Pro Unione has many interreligious and ecumenical resources that I have found helpful on my scholarly journey to gain more knowledge for the ministry in which God has entrusted me. It was exciting to see and participate in religious activities outside the United States of America. In Italy, my mind reflected on the time when my wife (Michelle) and I visited Haiti in 2001 with a combination of Duke University Divinity Students and Medical School Students. In Haiti we visited hospitals, schools, and churches. Michelle and I had the privilege once again to travel with Duke Divinity School (my alma mater) outside United States of America in the summer of 2004 upon returning from Italy, but this time we explored the schools, hospitals, and churches in Johannesburg and Capetown, South Africa. In Haiti and South Africa we had a great variety of religious and spiritual experiences with the people of their perspective land. A scholar on religion, Huston Smith wrote of his many experiences,

"The sermon in the service I attended this morning dwelt on Christianity as a world phenomenon. From mud huts in Africa to the Canadian tundra, Christians are kneeling today to receive the elements of the Holy Eucharist. It is an impressive picture. Still, as I listened with half my mind, the other half wandered to the wider company of God-seekers. I thought of the Yemenite Jews I watched six months ago in their synagogue in Jerusalem: dark-skinned men sitting shoeless and cross-legged on the floor, wrapped in the prayer shawls their ancestors wore in the desert... Swami Ramakrishna, in his tiny house by the Ganges at the foot of the Himalayas, will not speak today. He will continue the devotional silence that, with the exception of three days each year, he has kept for five years. By this hour U Nu is probably facing delegations, crises, and

cabinet meetings that are the lot of a prime minister, but from four to six this morning, before the world broke over him, he too was alone with the eternal in the privacy of the Buddhist shrine that adjoins his home in Rangoon. Dai Jo and Lai San, Zen monks in Kyoto, were ahead of him by an hour... What a strange fellowship this is, the God-seekers in every land, lifting their voices in the most disparate ways imaginable to the God of all life. How does it sound from above?..... (The World Religions, pg.1-2)

Smith asks a very good question about the sound we make from below. I suppose we will never know on this side of creation. However, I agree with Smith's statement in that **"All we can do is try to listen carefully and with full attention to each voice in turn as it addresses the divine." (Huston Smith, The World Religions, pg. 2)** And may I humbly add, as we listen to the voices of our sisters and brothers, may we also address the divine in our own special, unique, reverent style.

CHAPTER THREE
A PERSON IN A PASTOR

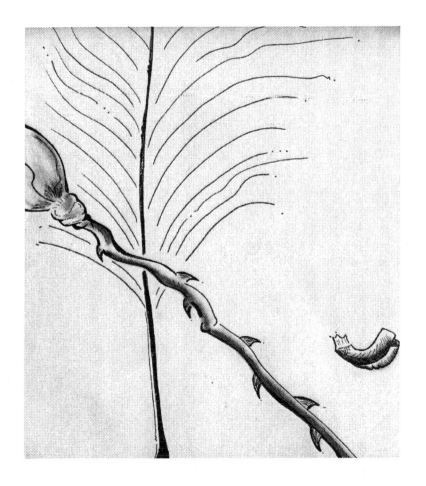

"You can not have a rose without thorns." -?

I VISITED HAITI AND HAITI VISITS ME

In 2001 I visited Haiti with a group of students from both Duke
University Divinity,
And Medical Schools.
Part of our mission was to bring hope,
But we quickly realized that the Haitians had lots of it,
Part of our mission was to inspire,
We concluded that the people were determined not to quit.

Geographically Haiti had striking similarities with Hawaii,
Which my wife and I visited a year later,
One of the major differences between Haiti and Hawaii was their
history,
The Haitians rebelled and kicked the invasive colonial powers off
their island,
The Hawaiians rebelled against the assailing colonial powers,
But were ultimately unsuccessful,
Haiti and Hawaii are dealing with the aftermath of their past
relationship,
With colonial powers.

A substantial amount of Hawaiians are still waiting for the government
to give them,
Back their land that was stolen;
However, they have lots of visitors and investors that keep them
company,
And have around 90% control financially, politically, and ownership
of the land,
Remember they lost the rebellion.
Haitians find it difficult to create a strong tourism component,
Visitors and global investors typically refuse to partner with Haiti to
promote growth,
Remember they won the rebellion.

In Haiti I visited the capital Port-au Prince with its crowded streets,
Hiked up Fondwas' mountains,
Attended church at a Sunday's worship service in City Sole,
Enjoyed music in Leogon,
Hugged, shook hands, cried, and kissed.

I saw beauty like never before,
In the midst of poverty that I never imagined,
I was both proud and ashamed of living in America,
Haiti visits me when I think of great potential against the odds,
A lonely warrior that was supposed to lose,
But continues fighting and refuses to give up.

A PASTOR NEEDS A PASTOR

You are responsible to preach, teach, pray, and counsel some,
Perform wedding ceremonies and eulogize the dead to name a few,
You must seek to release when your day is done,
For spiritual guidance, who are you going to?
A Pastor needs a Pastor, you must take care of you.

You need to listen to sermons rather than only hearing your own,
Do not bottle everything inside because you need someone to talk to also,
It is challenging, but do not take every problem from your vocation with you home,
For religious direction, who are you going to?
A Pastor needs a Pastor, you must take care of you.

The clergy journey can so easily be lonely and that is a fact,
It is unnecessary to attempt to carry the burdens by yourself,
You must find time to have fun and relax,
It is imperative to your health for you not to always be a Pastor, so who are you going to?
A Pastor needs a Pastor, you must take care of you.

EVERY TIME

Every goodbye is a tragic separation,
Every goodnight brings hope for another united tomorrow,
Every touch is as passionate as the first,
Every smile is bright as the sun,
Every sorrow is worst than the other,
Every argument is frightening,
Every kiss is a precious moment lost in time.

Every hug is a priceless phenomenon,
Every thought is as special as the other,
Every fantasy is desired to be reality,
Every prayer is as personal as the last,
Every song is as moving as the next,
Every sin distracts and hurts,
Every day is an opportunity for a new beginning.

EMOTIONAL CUT-OFF

I have to avoid your telephone calls and just let it ring... Too often I have placed the Phone to my ear and my heart followed, being left alone stranded on the line... No, I do Not want to hear your words and have a conversation... Your words are potent to my Internal system leaving me all shook up to the extent that my brain does not properly Function... Yes I do have to avoid your phone calls...

I can not see you or spend time with you... Every time I see you I see us and no matter How much time we spend together by my watch it is never enough... Looking into your Eyes shows me a future that will never come true... No, I should not see you or spend Time with you...

No communication is the best communication for us... Your letters to me tend to stay an Unhealthy amount of time before they get reluctantly thrown away... Your emails to me Usually somehow get saved, fill up my mailbox until I must erase them in order to go Forward in modernity and not get frozen in the past... I am too busy communicating to Myself that communicating with you is no good for me... That remains, no Communication is the best communication for us...

DISCRIMINATION

To be unaccepted is like a dagger through the spirit,
How can one go on as if nothing is wrong?
Support and assistance is a stranger,
Interferences and obstacles become comrades,
The feeling of sorrow turns into hate,
Why settle for injustice?
Wanting to express a violent outrage that is only found from the
bottomless pit.

How can one heal from the evil violation of another?
Only the celestial light can guide one to harmony,
The peaceful journey has an inferno path,
Remembering universality in creation is difficult when a person
opposes it,
Reaching for amazing grace for sinners such as I,
There must be a better place, but while I am here,
All of us have to wrestle with the term equality because I demand it
as well.

DEPRESSION

The calling of negative thought,
The insignificance of life itself,
Drowning in one's problems,
Crashing head-on in the sorrows of the world,
The acknowledged faults of oneself without rejuvenation,
The fading goals of oneself without a trace,
Happiness is lost miles away, and the horror of tomorrow is today.

NATURAL THINGS

The morning sunrise and stars shining bright at night in the sky,
Little kids playing in the rain and the sound of a young baby's cry,
Flowers blooming in the spring and the temperature dropping in the
winter,
Trick or treating in October and giving thanks in November,
A praying church and a faithful nun,
Planets constantly revolving around the sun,
These are natural things.

Poets writing, pilots flying, musicians playing an instrument,
People in love young or old continuously having letters sent,
A sailing ship, a racing car, a clock ticking away,
Bible verses, abstract paintings, waves floating all day,
Grass that grows, two eyes, two ears, and one nose,
I think, I wonder, I believe, and suppose,
These are natural things.

MOTHER NATURE

She provides homes for all her children,
But severely disciplines those who go against her rules,
Her beauty is adored and loved by all walks of life,
She speaks to me in many voices, and I treasure the time we spend
together alone,
All four of her temperamental seasons are delightful in their own
way,
Her decorations are overwhelming,
She possesses every need for everyone who lives with her to survive.

ONE MAN'S WISH UPON A STAR

If you come back and stay, my feelings for you will remain the same,
You in my arms will end this silent pain,
I still feel the same about you as I did the first day you left,
You are on my mind with every motion, every look, and every breath,
Maybe it's the way things should be, the two of us being apart,
I guess that's kool and everything, but first I'm gonna have to tell that to my heart,
In any case, wherever I am you will always have a friend.

Winter, spring, summer, fall, just call and I will be there,
A person has the right to dream and I heard they sometimes come true,
My dream has turned into a nightmare for me without you,
Do you know what you do to me when you are near and when you are not around?
Frowns transform into smiles, and smiles transform into frowns,
I want you to be by me and me where you are,
Maybe I am just one man with a wish upon a star.

ATLANTA'S WHISKEY

I drank in many cities, states, countries, and towns,
Delighted myself in a variety of rounds,
It could be the d.j.'s or j.d.'s,
Or occasional illusions of televiv,
There is something unique about Atlanta's whiskey.

Maybe Atlanta's colleges and universities are to blame,
There are too many to name,
Radio personalities on radio stations,
Singers, dancers, educators, hotty-tottys, entertainers, and other
occupations,
There is just something special about Atlanta's whiskey.

FATHER TO DAUGHTER

You must learn to break hearts, because many will come and leave,
You must learn to break hearts, because some will try to deceive,
You must learn to break hearts, because not everyone can have or take
you,
You must learn to break hearts, to not allow anyone the authority to
define,
Make or break you,
You must learn to break hearts, to protect yours my dear,
You must learn to break hearts, if you need me I will be there,
You must learn to break hearts, I am telling you this because I care.

You must love to learn how to do it yourself my love,
You must love to learn that there are times to embrace, push, and
shove,
You must love to learn to be able to not live in ignorance,
You must love to learn in order to be independent,
You must love to learn to continue to grow,
You must love to learn so anywhere in the world you can go,
You must love to learn to become more spiritually and physically rich
not poor.

You must know that I love you my daughter from beginning to no
end,
You must know God is our faithful, trusted savior, creator, and
friend,
You must know that I have tried to do for you all that I can,
You must know even though I am your father, I am still a human
man,
You must know that there is death in life and life after death,
You must know that I thought and think of you every day with every
breath,
You must know to remember this and never forget.

FATHER TO SON

You must work diligently, usually only headaches and heartaches are free,
You must work diligently in order to help provide for your family,
You must work diligently, read the Apostle Paul's advice to a congregation,
You must work diligently to continue to improve and uplift our nation,
You must work diligently, because idle time is the devil's workshop,
You must work diligently in whatever profession you choose to rise to the very top,
You must work diligently, you can pause, relax, have fun, but never completely stop.

You must respect women, because they are the vehicles of human life,
You must respect women for one is your mother, sister,
And another may become your wife,
You must respect women, although you may not agree with or like them all,
You must respect women, so open doors and pick them up when they tumble or fall,
You must respect women in order to be a gentleman,
You must respect women, then your flames will be easier to rekindle then,
You must respect women, so in order for you to do so you must not break,
But remember to bend.

You must know that I love you my son from beginning to no end,
You must know that God is our faithful, trusted savior, creator and friend,
You must know that I have tried to do for you all that I can,
You must know even though I am your father I am still a human man,
You must know that there is death in life and life after death,
You must know that I think of you every day with every breath,
You must know to remember this and never forget.

TROUBLE

One can get in trouble easily,
But it is difficult to get out,
Trouble may be fun doing,
In the end it can make you cry and shout,
It does not have any mercy,
Do not attempt to be its friend, because it will constantly drag you
down over,
And over again.

Sometimes it is very attractive, tempting,
Laborious to stay away from,
But you have to stay alert and never play dumb,
Trouble has nothing to lose but everything to gain,
It rarely forgets, forgives, and always makes space to collect more
names,
Do not let it catch you by yourself unaware,
Just stay away from it and have nothing to fear.

TIME

Time is the most valuable thing that a person can spend,
Time can get here in a second and be gone with the wind,
Time is something that does not come twice,
Time never freezes like ice,
Time should be treasured by all that encounter it,
Do not turn away from time, give up, or quit,
Stay, endure, keep trying, do not run, or split.

Time is always limited to everyone,
Time can be difficult,
Time can be fun,
Use time to the best of your ability,
Time is one of the few things you can get for free,
However, sometimes it can be expensive depending on where you
are,
Time gives you the opportunity to reach for the stars.

LOVE I ONCE KNEW

Damn, I needed her more than the oxygen I breathe,
She was my sun, but now I am in total darkness,
Her eyes are brighter than any star and her beauty is breath taking,
Holding her is holding love itself,
Being without her is torment,
I'm confined to loneliness that only she can break,
My heart is crushed by the mountain of pain.

I see her shadow in the sky, and I hear her voice in the wind,
I have only spent moments with her,
But I want to give her the rest of my life,
She is my definition of happiness,
And without her I can only feel sad,
She is the final piece to my puzzle,
Only then will my life be complete.

BOURBON STREET

I visited Bourbon Street, New Orleans while I was in undergraduate
school,
I remember walking down Bourbon Street as if it were yesterday,
All the alcoholic drinks and food for everyone,
People from all over the world visit New Orleans to walk on Bourbon
Street,
I wonder how many people have been seduced, by Bourbon Street's
temptations,
Young, old, rich, and poor people walking side by side,
Fascinated over the entertainment that Bourbon Street offers.

I wonder if Bourbon Street has changed peoples' lives permanently
after a visit,
Temporarily the people who visit Bourbon Street become one of her
own,
In one way or another through intoxication, dancing with strangers,
Only to be aroused for a moment,
Many visitors become victims of the camouflaged danger that New
Orleans possesses,
Many visitors' dreams come true if only for the time spent there,
Away from the realities of their daily lives,
Bourbon Street is a place in a time of its own,
People go there to visit, but many others go there to get away,
I wish to go back to New Orleans to walk on that street that the world
has traveled,
I plan to go to other places in the world,
I find pleasure in going to different places,
If my travels does not allow me to return,
The memory of the time spent there, takes me back to Bourbon
Street.

IT SHOULDA, WOULDA, COULDA, BUT, DIDN'T

Hey! Let me tell you about a boy who liked a girl. The girl liked him, but they couldn't get their act together to be with each other. You see she thought about him morning, noon, and night. He thought about her morning, noon, and night. They called each other and had great conversations, and admired each other's features. She talked; he talked, they day dreamed about each other. They wanted one another so they said. So you are asking, what was the problem? Other people I guess. The thought of what their friends would say. They thought of what other people would think.

Now you say well they didn't really like each other. Well they were young, in their late teens, and at that age peers have a great influence on one another. They missed out on a relationship that could have lasted. Who knows, it could have been the worst thing that had happened, but now it is too late to know. But is it too late? It is too late. It is over, and they did not even try or even try to start. They shoulda, woulda, coulda, but didn't. The boy and girl let their chances slip through their hands. Not because they wanted to, but rather how they thought it might turn out if their friends found out and did not approve. Is that silly or stupid? Is that good or is it just the way it is? Well, the boy shoulda, the girl woulda or coulda, but both of them didn't.

THE ANIMAL FROM WITHIN

Guilt thrashes against my heart while happiness leaves,
The isolation from the world comes to an end,
Many men fall from this feeling,
While many women oppose it,
The instinct of the animal comes creeping from within,
From the last hour of the last second the mind does not take control,
The flesh only knows what feels right and what is wrong only feels better.

The explanation of a reaction only the spirit can define,
The feeling of the killer instinct that boils at the bottom of the heart,
The heated temperature in your veins while you lose the only thing you ever wanted,
The experience that only the pale moon light witnesses,
The flashback of the moment that makes your body chill,
The silent howl in the stillness of time,
Comes from the animal from within.

I THOUGHT OF YOU

I thought of you and my heart skipped a beat,
My face formed a smile,
My muscles relaxed,
My mind went down memory lane,
I saw the sun shining bright, blue skies, stars at night; held hands,
Tight hugs, long conversations,
Flowers blooming, birds chirping, your sweet fragrance in the air,
My ears heard faint whispers in the wind that said, "I miss you,"
"I love you", and "Can we do that again?"

I thought of you and my mind continued to go down memory lane,
Clouds started to cover the sun and the stars lost their sparkle,
My stomach cringed and my face crinkled,
Flowers faded, birds became silent,
Voices of anger, disappointment, insults, and lies echoed in my ears,
My eyes glimpsed tears, a frown, and a body language of mistrust,
I thought of you and was happy that my mind forgot.

I CAN NOT HOLD MY HEART

I can not hold my heart,
Tell me, can you hold yours?
Every time I think I have it, my heart goes walking, jogging, or running out of the door,
It seems to never learn its lesson, no matter how broken it gets,
My heart gets tossed around, thrown away, bumped, bruised,
I suppose somehow it always forgets,
About the pain, confusion, frustration, and loneliness, to name a few.

Sometimes I feel as if my heart is the only one,
So tell me, does this ever happen to you?
Does your heart keep still, keep silent, and keep to itself on your command?
I wish mine did, because I so diligently try my best,
It usually gets the upper hand,
It usually denies my several requests,
Do you understand?

My heart takes me through changes even when I try to refuse,
At various times it puts me in tune with rap, country, classical, jazz,
All sorts of rhythms and all kinds of blues,
Maybe one day I will master the art,
To not allow my heart to get stolen, creep, run, or fly away in the air as if it were a dart,
Until I succeed I will keep trying. I will not quit, because it belongs to me from the start,
Tell me if you find the secret, because I can not hold my heart.

ASSOCIATE PASTORS

You seldom have the last word, but you do most of the work that no one wants to do,
Anniversaries, accolades, and dinner invitations are seldom extended to you,
But you still work when your hands turn black and blue,
It is almost as if you are sailing by a cruise boat and you are sailing up stream in a canoe,
You usually do not get to preach often, or get other invitations to speak,
Yet few people notice that you are at the church the most during the week,
Known as a jack of all trades, but none expected to master the life of Associate Pastors.

Depending on your congregation you may perform many weddings.
You try to keep a low profile, not be a rebel rouser, or do too much meddling,
Sometimes looked upon as simply extra help, and at times that can hurt a great deal,
Having always to protect your heart and feelings with the holy armor and shield,
Trying to find your proper role and be effective in it,
Some days contemplating giving up, giving out, or simply quitting,
Rarely getting credit for victories while cleaning up disasters,
The life of Associate Pastors.

Associate Pastors are not equivalent to Senior Pastors, but do more than most laity,
If their words carry as much weight as the Senior Pastor that is a rarity,
If they get just as much vacation or time off that is surprising,
If their salary gets close to the Senior Pastor it may start an uprising,
Yet Associate Pastors are wanted to do various chores,
Greet people as they walk in and out of the church, then open and close doors,
Going in such a fast pace, as if racing in a nascar race,
The life of Associate Pastors.

YOUNG TO OLD, OLD TO YOUNG

Two people met and took an insightful view,
One young, one old, both accomplished in their own way,
One said "Hi" and the other asked "How do you do?"
They agreed that they would not have gotten as far as they have if they did not daily pray,
They gazed at one another in admiration and thought some things through.

The young informed the old,
"I look at you with envious eyes because of all you have done,
I respect your experience, knowledge, and wisdom,
For what you have endured I say, 'Congratulations,'
I suppose you learned to talk less and do more listening,
What were some of your triumphs, victories, loses, and tribulations?"
The old gently smiled at the young and gave the following reply,
"I look at you with eyes full of excitement with anticipation of what you can do,
Your brain is young, flexible enough now to grasp the world in which we live,
Triumphs, victories, loses, and tribulations come to all,
But remember that God is able to see and carry you through,
Most of your life is ahead of you while mine is past with little more to give,
One of the most important decisions you will have make is to live your life positively."
Eager to answer and to get some advice, the young answered the old,
"I do want to positively effect the world without it negatively affecting me,
I desire to be a shining star in whatever profession I choose,
I know some days will be turbulent, but I will have more full of tranquility,
I expect numerous battles, so tell me how to win more than I lose,
I do not want to halfheartedly live, so what can I do to experience life completely?"
The old pondered the questions then responded to the young,

"Allow yourself and the world to change one another because both have lots to share,
Keep reaching to be a shining star, most do not make it because they simply quit,
For those days you think are turbulent or tranquil, just know that God is there,
Most battles are not intended to win or lose, the importance is to fight a lot or a little bit."
The young quickly asked the old more questions, knowing that they would soon depart,
"If you could change anything in your life, what would it be?
What are some mistakes to avoid?
Do you think I can ever be as successful as you, a person like me?
Are all my questions getting you annoyed?
I appreciate your time and answers sincerely."
The old shook the young hand gave a pat on the back then said,
"I would not change anything in my life, because I have learned from everything,
Live your life, because once you are dead- you are dead,
Then on that good old morning we all will see the King."

A BLESSED MAN

Her absence leaves me with emptiness,
Everyday without her brings hours of torment,
I am dependent on her touch,
I am lost without her eyes,
The sound of her heartbeat eases my soul,
I gravitate towards her physically and spiritually,
She helps me pray to God.

Her companionship is a blessing in my life,
I am mesmerized by her kiss and a prisoner in her arms,
My heart is drowning by a burning passionate love,
I need air but my oxygen resides in her lungs,
She is my helpmate sent from up above,
I gravitate towards her intimately and religiously.
She helps me pray to God.

FOR A PASTOR'S WIFE (ESPECIALLY MINE)

A lovely face with a gentle smile, with patience that is stretched for miles,
Having to set her family's schedule around an organization consisting of several people,
Sentimental to some situations, but not transparent or being able to be seen through,
Waiting for extended conversations, church activities,
And various visitations to be through,
Staying by her husband through prayer, hoping it will act as glue.

Sharing her husband who is the minister to, and for people who vie for his attention,
Sometimes disappointed, unhappy, irate, but alert not to show any contention.
Religion should ideally be liberating, but you sometimes feel like you are in detention,
Rarely in the spotlight or getting standing ovations,
Every day would not be enough for her husband to show her sincere appreciation.

She gives encouragement, inspiration, and support in so many ways,
When everyone else goes home, attacks, or insults, she remains and stays,
Giving words of comfort and illustrating behavior that eases,
Praying for me and helping me stand when I fall down on my knees,
Thank you for being my toughest critic and my biggest fan- never stop doing that please.

ACKNOWLEDGEMENTS

I thank God for grace and mercy upon my life. Much love goes to my parents for always affirming my dreams. I also thank my wife Michelle who has displayed an extraordinary amount of patience and support during the completion of this book. I sincerely appreciate William Willimon writing the foreword for my first book. Most importantly, Will, I appreciate our friendship, your mentoring, assistance, and the unselfish sharing of your wisdom with me. I am also grateful to Douglass Fitch for writing the introduction for my first book. However, Doug, I am most grateful for your friendship, your mentoring, assistance, and the unselfish sharing of your wisdom with me. Sincere gratitude also goes to Vernell Wilson from True Life Publications who gave timely advice. I dare not name any more people in fear that I will inadvertently omit others that contributed to this writing project. Last but not least, special blessings to all the churches, pastors, parishioners, schools, and teachers who have encouraged me along the way- the best is yet to come!

Grace and Peace,

K. J. W.

Kenny J. Walden

Printed in the United States
37575LVS00007B/46-51